Up in the sky

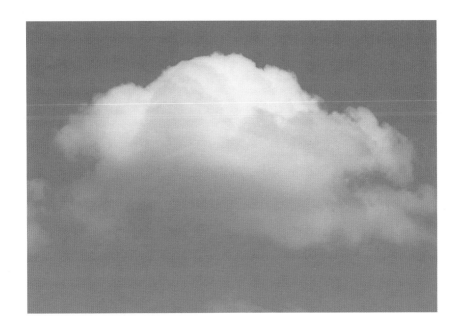

The balloon is up in the sky.

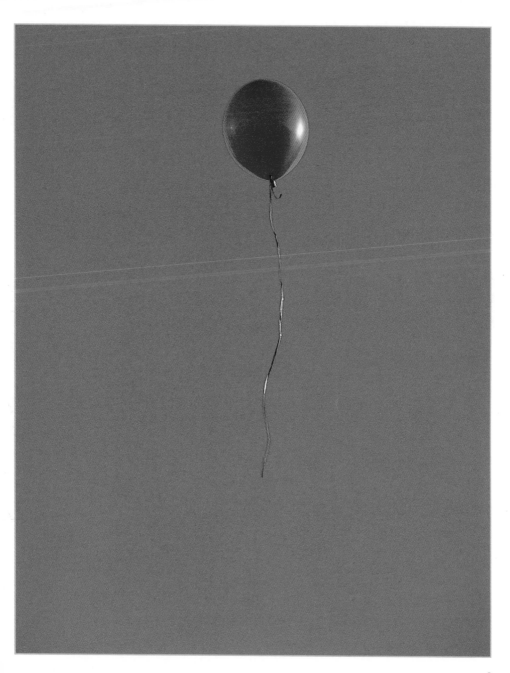

The kite is up

in the sky.

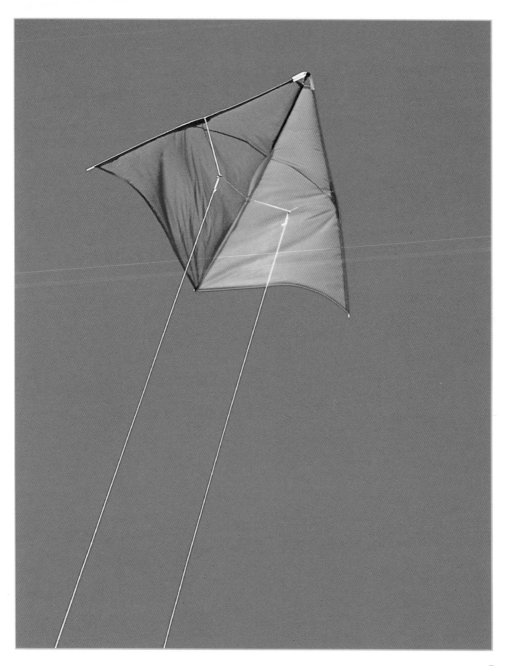

5

The bird is up

in the sky.

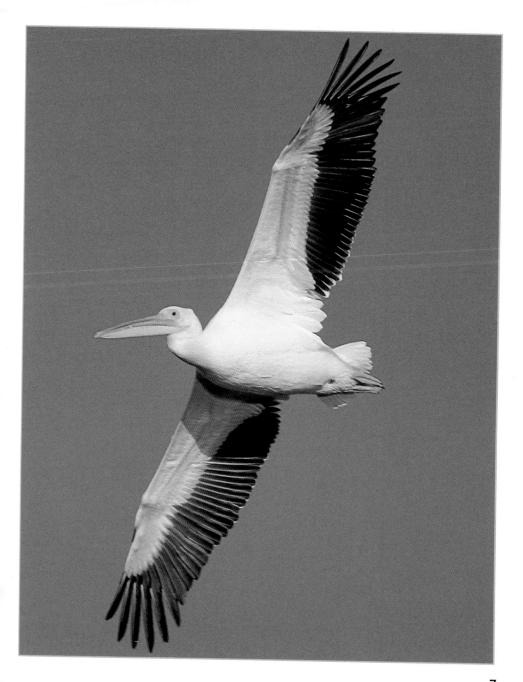

The helicopter is up

in the sky.

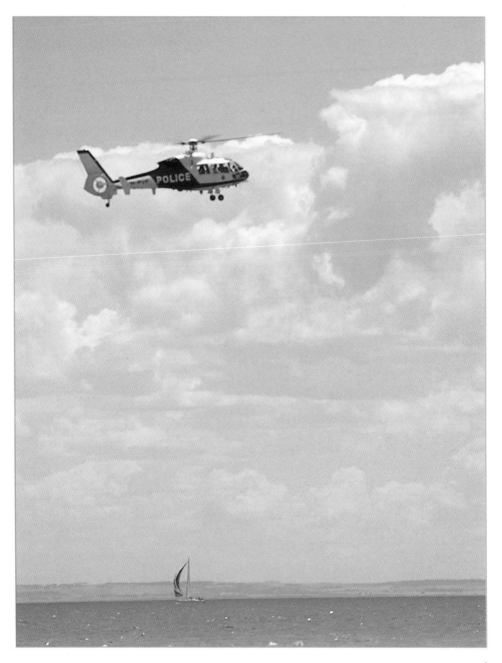

The plane is up

in the sky.

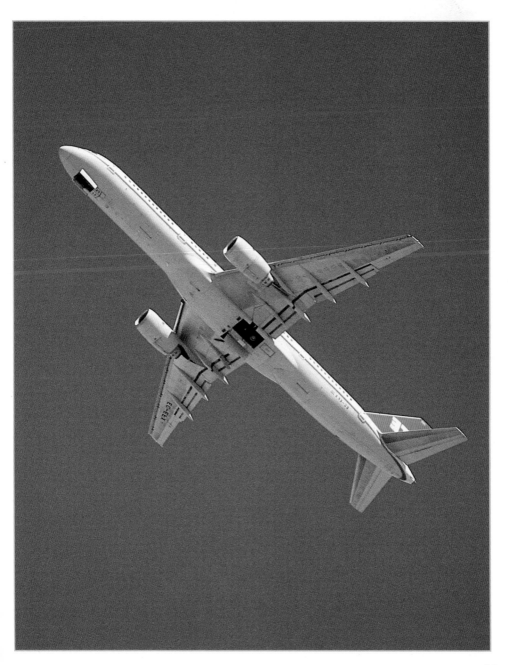

The cloud is up

in the sky.

The rainbow is up

in the sky.

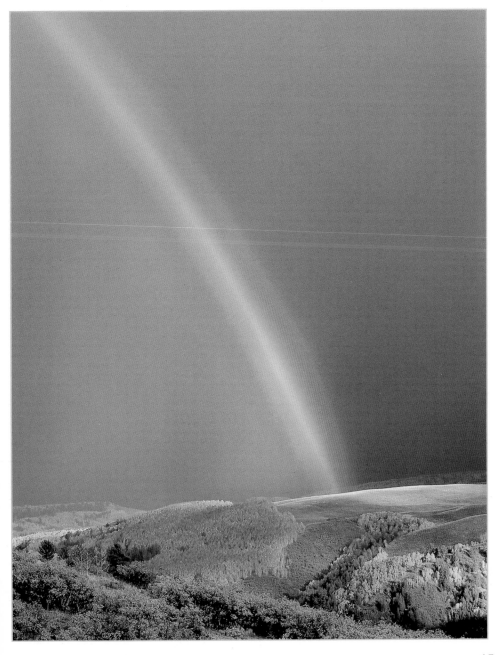

The sun is up

in the sky.

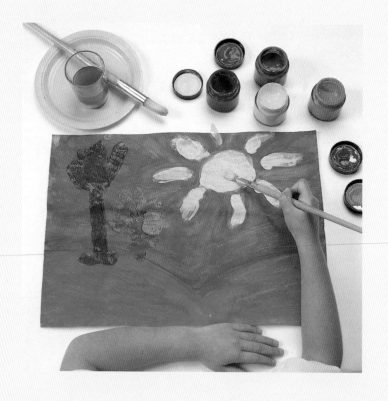